AF255210

Advance Praise for *TRAPPED*

This book is a must read! It reaches the soul of who we are at our most vulnerable state and helps us to understand the power within us. Brandon Holt, your book is powerful and will help many others on their journey.

—Miranda Bouldin,
President/CEO, LogiCore, Huntsville, AL

Read this powerful book if you need a guide on how to liberate yourself from past pain and dangerous narratives that wreak havoc in your life by realizing your own capacity to pursue positive self-growth and the promise of hope.

—Dr. Janet Taylor, Psychiatrist,
Cognitive Health & Wellness, Bradenton, FL

TRAPPED

TRAPPED

BRANDON HOLT, LCDC

TABLE OF CONTENTS

FOREWORD

Like most of us, my brother Brandon strives for perfection, but like all of us, he falls short. It's the authentic leaders who separate themselves from the rest when willing to expose character defects hoping to bring healing to the world. I've been very fortunate in my life to see some measures of success from a professional, personal, and spiritual standpoint. I've worked in corporate board rooms, nonprofit offices, and political circles and have seen many leaders rise and fall. The world is not an easy place. People, for the most part, have good intentions, but the pressures of life always find its way of building you up but also tearing you down.

In Brandon's first book, *Preaching Under the Influence: A Minister's Struggle,* he describes his journey from rock bottom to recovery. *TRAPPED* presents a roadmap for those dealing with personal struggles that you desire to conquer. Several people have issues of anger, insecurities, and a false sense of what we think reality should be. This book allows you to rip off the visible mask seen by others and confront the real person in the mirror. It's a simple yet deep look into how we should move forward. I applaud my brother for continuing to expose himself and his setbacks so that those who are afraid to address their challenges can hopefully do so and know that they're not alone. We all have vices, some major, some minor but we have to find a way to cope with those vices. This masterpiece is another step in that direction.

David C. Lews
Brother to the author

INTRODUCTION

Last year, I published a book about life under the influence of toxic substances such as drugs and alcohol. I shared my past addiction to prescription pills and how it affected my life. After a terrible car accident that led to a necessary surgery, I was prescribed painkillers to help cope. The recommended dosage turned into a couple more, which turned into a handful more, which turned into my needing them for more than the physical pain, which turned into my joining the 3.3 million other Americans who misuse prescription painkillers.

My addiction led to me losing almost everything, including my role as a pastor, my family, and nearly my life. Fortunately, I was able to turn my situation around. In doing so, I recovered much of what I had lost in my journey through addiction. Afterward, I had the choice to keep what I'd gone through private; to relocate, put it all behind me, and pretend that it never happened. That wasn't my choice, however. I learned how many people were affected by the same issue—directly and indirectly—and knew that I had to do something. I had to tell my story.

After opening up and recommitting myself to God, my wife, my family, and my sense of purpose, I opened up to my congregation as well. I extended my sharing by counseling in the local prison and eventually writing a book. I felt called to reach as many people as I possibly could with my struggle and the solution—the truth—according to my experiences. A major component of that struggle and solution was identifying the root of the problem. Addiction doesn't just happen. It attached itself to what already existed inside of me, to battles that I had successfully covered up yet hadn't defeated. To overcome my dependence on pills, I also needed to address the root issues that had led to my addiction—the primary ones being anger, denial, and a desire for acceptance, states of being that I'd carried with me since childhood. Over time, they slowly hardened until I felt trapped.

I realized that I wasn't the only one suffering from character defects such as anger, code switching, miscommunication, and more. Just as I had shared my painful story of overcoming addiction to painkillers, I felt the same sense of urgency to share my journey of navigating the roadblocks that affected me and prevented me from living my best life. After all, drugs and alcohol aren't the only influences that we can be trapped beneath. That's why I decided to write this book: to equip and motivate those who aren't feeling fulfilled in their life's purpose, those who are lacking success or satisfaction in their relationships, those who are falling short of overcoming the burden of anger, and those who are just tired of feeling trapped.

Feeling trapped can be a frustrating or even terrifying place to be in life, as it forces us to analyze our present reality. For some of us, it goes back to childhood experiences. There's always this sense of wanting more, yet never having been able to reach it. For others, it creeps up on you. Everything was going well, then bam! Conflict happened, or maybe something didn't happen that should have, and suddenly you realize that something has to change in your life, immediately. If you're anything like me, you probably spend (or spent) most of your time trapped in thoughts of the past, trapped in the present reality, or trapped daydreaming or worrying about a future that isn't even guaranteed. When we feel trapped, we're usually focused on everything but the present.

When we reach this point of feeling trapped, we may ask ourselves: Should I change careers? Leave my relationship? Relocate to a new residence? Seek therapeutic assistance? Being trapped shows up when our desired outcome conflicts with our present reality, but we (most likely) are intimidated by the thought of making the necessary changes. And we're afraid to make those changes because of that infamous fear of the unknown. What will change require of you? We don't know, so we stay in the same frustrating position. We jam our emotions further inside of us, where they turn into stress, unsettled thoughts, anxiety, and a number of physical ailments—all of which can ultimately lead to addiction.

As a licensed chemical dependency counselor who has worked in a wide range of treatment domains, I have assisted clients who were determined to confront and resolve the internal and external conflicts they'd been battling. When we discussed being trapped under the influences of anger, rigid belief systems, communication issues, codependency, code switching, fear of the unknown, and thinking errors, I witnessed the seed of hope being planted. Reaching character growth is a work in progress for any individual—husband, wife, father, teenager, pastor, coach, educator, executive, and more. These principles that I discuss in this book have sparked change, from within prison walls to within the pews of the church, and if you're open to receiving and applying them, they will work for you, too.

Chapter 1
Trapped Under the Influence of Anger

The Merriam-Webster Learner's Dictionary defines anger as "a strong feeling of being upset or annoyed because of something wrong or bad" (www.learnersdictionary.com/definition/anger). We determine that something is "wrong or bad" when expectations are not met, and when belief systems are violated. Core belief systems are established through what we taste, touch, see, hear, and smell, as well as through experiences that we encounter through our environment, family, social connections, education, or vocation, to name a few. Anger is not about a situation, but rather has to do with our belief about the situation. When our perceived truth is violated, our irrational defense mechanisms arise.

I've had a fierce, raging, compulsive temper from a really young age, and because of it I've harmed several close relationships, especially with the people who loved me the most. I recall my basketball playing days in Arlington, Texas, getting into several heated altercations jockeying for position "in the paint," hoping to rebound a missed shot. I also remember getting kicked off the varsity basketball team in eleventh grade because of it. I had a lot of pent-up resentment from childhood experiences, from being biracial and experiencing bullying. The first time I remember being bullied, it involved a guy in seventh grade throwing me against a locker because I wouldn't give him my Nestle Crunch candy bar. When he did that, it birthed a belief in me that I needed to protect myself at all times when feeling threatened.

As John Maxwell says in his book *21 Irrefutable Laws of Leadership*, hurt people hurt people. Additionally, a lot of that hurt usually stems from unmet needs and expectations, such as a parent demonstrating favoritism for one sibling over another. We are disappointed that our parents and guardians failed to acknowledge our very existence. We are disappointed that our teachers and other school staff didn't validate our educational progress. We are disappointed in a friend or family member who noticeably refused to celebrate our success. Consequently, we turn to anger. This was certainly the case for me, and while becoming angry was not a conscious thing, it happened nonetheless.

Unrealistic expectations are premeditated resentment and, without fail, lead to shattered self-esteem and disappointment, which in turn leads to anger. Why does this happen? It happens because disappointment leads to a sense of having a lack of power, or a sense of impotence, or a sense simply of disempowerment. In that sense of disempowerment is a feeling of having no control over what happened, and wherever disempowerment exists, so does anger. We may not always be immediately aware of it, but it's often the case.

When a person feels disempowered, often the only way for them to feel empowered again is through anger and control. Not only does the adrenaline release that is triggered by anger make you feel dominant and powerful, anger is also powerfully effective in substituting for whatever pain you're actively trying to avoid. Being mad rather than in pain has its benefits, the main one being distraction. When you're in emotional pain, your mind is consumed with it. It's all you think about, and it gets to the point where you feel it physically. But when you're angry, you deflect your internal rage toward the person you're angry with. However, without using effective anger management strategies, internal rage can quickly turn into external retaliation. Even if it isn't a physical lashing out, you want them to feel what you feel. Remember, hurt people hurt people.

The alchemy of pain into anger involves a shift in attention from yourself to someone else. Therefore, anger is like a bandage, temporarily protecting you from having to acknowledge and deal with the underlying hurt. The spouse who resents getting married will find it easier to lash out at their partner about every little thing instead of confronting their own mistake and taking action to turn the situation around. Being angry helps you hide the reality of being afraid or feeling vulnerable, and, more importantly, it creates a sense of righteousness that doesn't exist when you're simply in pain.

When my bully slammed me against the locker, I felt powerless. I felt vulnerable. When my loved ones decided they had had enough of the verbal attacks that I dished out during my addiction and ceased communicating with me, I felt powerless and vulnerable. So, to avoid feeling vulnerable then as a child and today as an adult, I became angry and strongly believed myself to be justified in that anger.

Your issues follow you wherever you go. If left unchecked, anger travels with you. The anger that started in my childhood followed me into my teenage years, on through college, and into my adult life. Five percent of our anger has to do with the situation, and the other 95 percent has to do with our belief about the situation. Let's use the example of road rage. You're driving down the freeway and someone cuts you off, and you verbally abuse them through explicit language, despite the fact that you'll probably never see this person again. Five percent of your anger has to do with the fact that the person cut you off. The other 95 percent points back to an unresolved issue from your past. Maybe you were cut off as a child a lot, or witnessed your parents cut each other off, so you've developed a belief system that it is wrong or bad to cut someone off. Therefore, the person that cuts you off today is the relatively innocent recipient of your aggression, but the underlying issue stems from failure to address your unhealthy belief system . We call that the 5/95 Rule.

There's no one approach to dealing with anger because there are various manifestations of it. So, before we get into solutions, let's first explore the different types of anger. While there are far more types of anger than I list here, these are the most common ones:

- Explosive Anger

- Chronic Anger

- Hidden Anger

- Incidental Anger

Explosive Anger

Explosive anger, which can also be called acute anger, can make a person into a rage-aholic. This person gets a euphoric high when they go off. Every situation is a major incident. Interactions with people are hostile. The least little issue sets them off into a volcanic reaction. This anger is unpredictable, unleashing rage at a moment's notice. They shoot from zero to ten in a matter of seconds when someone violates their core belief system. When they explode, they get a sense of that dominant, alpha, unconquerable energy, and when they come back down, they often feel guilt, shame, and remorse. They'll produce alligator tears, waves of apologies, and dozens of flowers. A lot of abusers, physical abusers especially, have what is called explosive anger.

Childhood is a critical time in our development. It's during this time that we learn about interpersonal relationships and how to manage our emotions. Experiencing trauma during childhood can disrupt the process of learning emotion management. As a result, children grow into teenagers and adults who may not have adequately learned how to manage their emotions or negotiate interpersonal relationships. So when anger shows up, people with a history of childhood trauma may not know how to control or release those emotions, resulting in strong anger impulses and destructive behavior. This was the case with me. I was never good at concealing it and just dealing with it. I always let it out; I was very explosive.

My dad used to always tell me, "One day that's going to catch up with you." You know, you get frustrated with a situation, your thinking becomes irrational, you get explosive, you lash out. My dad would tell me, "You're going to do something and it's going to have consequences." I would get mad, explosively mad, and say something or do something, but then I would come back and apologize. But after too many apologies, people tend to cut you off, and they don't want to deal with you anymore.

A few ways that explosive anger shows up are:

- Shouting

- Cursing

- Road rage

- Blaming others

- Physical abuse

- Throwing things

- Breaking things

- Slamming doors

People who explode when angry have bouts of aggressive, violent behavior or angry verbal outbursts that are out of proportion to the situation at hand. It might be the father who throws a plate at the wall because the dishes aren't washed, for instance, or the kid who throws the remote control at the television because he lost the video game. Their anger is out of proportion. While explosive anger shows up predominantly in males and in those who are suffering from substance abuse problems, it is not limited to them. Females demonstrate these behaviors as well, as do those who are sober and always have been. If you exhibit repeating occurrences of explosive anger, I recommend professional help, which can range from finding help online to taking in-person anger management courses, as this can be a sign of intermittent explosive disorder.

Explosive anger is dangerous. Both the person who's angry and those around them are put at risk of being harmed, personal property is at risk of being damaged, and relationships are made fragile and difficult to maintain. Because it's so dangerous, it should never be tolerated as an acceptable form of anger. It's not healthy and shouldn't be treated as such. If you're the parent of a child who expresses explosive anger, the spouse of a partner who does, the child of a parent, the employee of a supervisor, etc., protect yourself from this behavior, especially if you are being physically abused.

Chronic Anger

Chronic anger is characterized by ongoing anger that seemingly never lets up. This person wakes up angry, goes to bed angry, and responds angrily, usually before they even know the full extent of what was said or done. Those with chronic anger see the world through a narrow red filter. They are highly reactive to situations and likely exhibit explosive anger. Rarely do they take the time to think about what's going on around them and within them. Instead of self-reflection, they tend to blame others. Because they never take the time to get to the root of their issue, the cycle is ongoing. If nothing changes, nothing changes. Situations stack on top of situations, the anger continues to fester, and their likelihood of satisfying their wants and needs is stuck on pause.

While it is possible for explosive anger to show up only in one place, most likely at home, chronic anger is pervasive. There's no hiding it. The resentment is evidenced on the job, at home, and every day in comings and goings. Their habitual irritation and frustration is ever present, reflected on the person's resting face, in their aura, and in their voice. You don't have to see them to know they have an "attitude problem." Most frequently, it comes from old wounds rooted in some kind of emotional or physical abuse or neglect that have yet to be healed. It can also be rooted in feelings of powerlessness regarding relationships, health, money, or social status.

While some people who suffer from chronic anger can pinpoint exactly what the root cause of their ongoing anger is, others may fail to associate that root with their anger. Either way, however, some may embrace chronic anger as an emotional guard intended to protect them from pain. Chronic anger, for instance, can help us avoid, once again, the self-reflection necessary for personal development. It can serve to dodge the difficulty of pondering questions related to who we really are (the person beneath the hurt), what our purpose in life is, and what gives our life meaning.

Until we begin to address those questions, we're living our lives on autopilot, letting our emotions—hurt, mainly—lead the way. While on autopilot, we're reactive to situations instead of contemplative about situations. It's a way to avoid self-responsibility by blaming instead. And this isn't the "having a bad day because my boss said something disrespectful to me at work" kind of blaming. It's "my father wasn't there for me growing up, so I resent all men," or, "my grandmother called me ugly names, so I'm forever bitter and resentful, believing that everyone who looks at me thinks the same thoughts that my grandmother did," or, "my ex-wife left me for someone else, and now I no longer find joy in anything."

It's easier to hold onto the anger than to do the inner work (and possibly even have the necessary confrontation) to heal it. Holding on feels like it protects us—and in some ways, it does. However, it also deprives us. You can liken it to being the president of the United States. With your secret service around, you're pretty safe from outside harm (not completely safe, but definitely safer). Yet you're also deprived of many simple pleasures, like being able to walk down the street alone or enjoy the privacy of your entire house to yourself.

Because chronic anger leads you to believe that no one is to be trusted, you won't fully open up to anyone emotionally. This prevents relationships from deepening to any level of meaningfulness. It also obstructs our ability to forgive others when they do make mistakes. It's as if the mistake was expected, bound to happen. For the record, I'm not trying to invalidate the hurt at all. Nor am I suggesting that there really isn't anyone to blame. I'm only saying that, at some point, you have to let it go, move on, and take some here-on-out responsibility.

The refusal to set our anger aside and let our guard down, to recognize our hurt and embrace the grieving process, can keep us trapped under the influence of anger. We remain stuck, frozen in time, with little to no chance for change or growth. Instead of fulfillment and growth, chronic anger promises us only more disempowerment and disappointment. It's like procrastinating. In doing so, you're temporarily satisfied because you're putting off doing the work, but it's not sustainable. Chronic anger works the same way by distracting us from our role in the problem, keeping us trapped in time.

I'm eternally inspired by veterans and athletes who lose a limb and find a way to keep going. They could've easily and almost understandably given up and spent the rest of their lives in front of the television, chronically angry. Instead, they decline disempowerment, rediscover their reason for living, and keep moving. It's important for all of us to maintain that same energy, to continue strengthening our will in the face of adversity.

Hidden Anger

Hidden anger can be difficult to "diagnose," because it's . . . hidden. You're upset, you just haven't said so. It's likely because you haven't acknowledged it to yourself, either. Hidden anger tends to originate in childhood, too. If, as a child, you weren't allowed to express your anger without punishment, then you're more likely to grow up with hidden anger, which is rooted in fear. A person who is recognition deprived, lacks approval, is overlooked in school, or witnesses parental favoritism toward a sibling has the tendency to lock down their true feelings inside themselves.

Instead of speaking up about what upset you, you might say something sarcastic or roll your eyes behind the person's back. Hidden anger can be just as internally dangerous as explosive anger is externally harmful. Whenever you keep intense emotions bottled up, it's eating away at you. Your body will be tense and will likely exhibit symptoms like tics, clenched jaws, tight shoulders and hips, etc. Because your body is trapped in flight-fight-freeze mode, that's where all its resources are going. As a result, your immune system is weakened, increasing your chances for illnesses and diseases. Hidden anger is concealed inside of you. It is like a sealed pot that is boiling. Eventually, it is going to explode if you don't turn the pot off.

Hidden anger is caused by something that you have been holding on to and can manifest itself in several ways. In "Getting to the Root of Hidden Anger," an article for *Psychology Today*, Dr. Gregory L. Jantz, behavioral and mental health disorder specialist, identified eight ways that hidden anger shows up. Some you might find surprising. I provide an example with each manifestation of hidden anger:

- Procrastination: Your partner gives you a list of tasks that need to be done around the house. Because you're upset, you drag your feet in getting the job done. Another way that hidden anger leads to procrastination is due to the distraction of anger. You can be so mentally and emotionally occupied with the target of your anger that you have no capacity for the task at hand.

- Habitual lateness: You might either be late everywhere you go or you're late to certain places (usually the ones you despise having to be). Someone who is chronically angry, for instance, is perhaps always late. As a result, they have to rush, provoking road rage and an even nastier attitude upon arrival. If you hate your job, on the other hand, you're probably more likely to only show up late there. If you dislike your family, you're likely to only show up late to family functions.

- Sarcasm, cynicism, or flippancy: When you're around certain people or are in certain environments, you always have something sarcastic to say. Someone likely tends to remark that you always have something smart to say. You also always have negative remarks to say about the situation that you pass off as truth— no optimism.

- Frequent sighing: This is a subtle one, marked by impatience and irritability. Everything gets on your nerves, and because you can't say or do what's really on your mind, you let out a deep, loud exhale instead.

- Smiling while hurting: This one aligns with Chapter 5, where I will talk about masks. You're smiling on the outside, but inside you're hurting, you're angry, you're discontent. The smile is your way of hiding how you truly feel. After the person walks away, your smile disappears just as fast as it appeared.

- Frequent disturbing or frightening dreams: You keep having the same dream of falling into a deep, dark hole. It seems so real, as you can feel the butterflies in your stomach and the sense that there's no end to the fall. Dreams have a way of revealing what rests in the subconscious, allowing you to contend with deep emotions like anger, fear, and sadness.

- Excessive irritability over trifles: Someone cuts you off in traffic and you let them have it. You're cursing and honking and trying to get as close as you possibly can to let them know that you don't appreciate their maneuver. Minor inconveniences really send you over the edge.

- Unconscious physical movements: These may be facial tics, spasmodic foot movements, habitual fist clenching, or similar repeated physical acts that are done unintentionally. This is one of the signs that you might not even be aware of. The tension of these movements, however, might cause frequent headaches.

Incidental Anger

Incidental anger is a healthy, in-the-moment response to something that happened to you that upset you. Maybe someone cut you off in traffic and almost hit you. With incidental anger, you honk your horn and spew a few words, then let it go. Moving on is the key. Unlike chronic anger, you don't allow these feelings to linger. It happened and, if possible, you dealt with it, and then you moved on. You don't wake up angry or see red for nothing that you can actually pinpoint. You know exactly what occurred. But while incidental anger is healthy, it's important to maintain mindfulness during episodes of it, lest it become explosive or chronic.

I want to share one of my favorite stories of mindfulness with you:

There was a man and a child. The boy said, "I saw you on TV. I want to be successful, just like you."

The man said, "Are you sure you want to be successful?"

The boy said, "Yes, sir."

The man said, "I want you to meet me at the lake at three o'clock in the morning."

"Yes, sir," the boy answered. The next morning, he got there at 2:45 am because he was hungry for success. He was hungry to be great.

The man walked out there and saw the boy was already there. He said, "All right, you sure you want to be successful?"

The boy said, "Yes, sir."

"Are you positive?" the man asked.

"Yes, sir," the boy said.

So the man said, "I want you to walk three steps into the water with me."

The boy agreed and they walked out there, the water up to their ankles. The man asked again, "Are you sure you want to be successful, young fella?"

"Yes, sir."

They walked out ten more feet and the water was up to their waists. The man asked a fourth time, "Are you sure you want to be successful?"

"Yes, sir." So they kept walking until the water was up to their chests. The man asked a fifth time, "Are you sure you want to be successful?"

This time, the boy asked, "Sir, what does this have to do with success?"

"Do you want to be successful or not?" the man asked.

"Yes, sir."

They walked out until the water was up to the boy's mouth, angering him, because he didn't know how to swim. The man asked again, "Do you want to be successful?"

Again the boy answered, "Yes, sir."

"Are you sure you want to be successful?"

"Yes, sir."

As they walked, the man took the boy and slammed him underneath the water and held him under. The boy was kicking and shaking and fighting the man. Finally, when the man felt the boy slow down, he jerked his head back out of the water. The boy emerged, ready to fight him. He asked the man, "What's wrong with you? What were you doing? What were you thinking?"

The man shrugged and answered, "I thought you wanted to be successful."

The boy said, "I did, but that had nothing to do with success."

The man asked, "When you were underneath that waterline, what were you thinking about? Were you thinking about your family?"

"No."

"Were you thinking about your job?"

"No."

"Were you thinking about school?"

"No."

"Were you thinking about your social life?"

"No."

He asked the boy, "What were you thinking about?"

The boy responded, "The only thing I was thinking about was my next breath."

In life, that's how you have to be when you're trapped. You have to be in the moment. It's called mindful meditation. You have to be in the moment; not yesterday, not tomorrow, in the moment. Because when you're in the moment, you are focused on the matter that is at hand. The only thing that should be important to you is what's going on right here, right now.

Roadmap to Victory

Anger may be an unpleasant, inconvenient emotion to deal with, but it's normal, healthy, and even necessary. It lets us know that something isn't right, that something needs to change, and it can be a powerful motivating force in provoking that change.

Each type of anger carries different weights. Explosive, acute anger is the most noticeable. It's what comes to mind first when we think of anger. It's the hole in the wall after someone's punched it, the brick through a window, a black eye on someone's face. It's the 911 call because things have gotten out of hand.

It's loud, insulting words that can't be taken back. Chronic anger is an emotion that has been lingering for a while and can very well be explosive at times. Chronic anger, in general, changes a personality. It's what people associate with you—because you tend to be negative or pessimistic most of the time, tending to see the worst in things, seeing the proverbial cup as half empty instead of half full—and that bitterness affects your relationships. There's also hidden anger, where you want to not ruffle feathers or risk abandonment, so you don't address the problem head-on, but you still carry that burden. And finally, you have incidental anger, which is being upset at a specific situation, but which you can let go of after the moment has passed.

Again, anger is normal and necessary, but unfortunately, most of us have never been taught how to manage it. We learn to ignore it, suppress it, or even allow it to consume us, but rarely do we learn how to deal with it in a positive way. Because uncontrolled anger can take a toll on our health and relationships, it's critical to adopt coping skills for addressing anger, such as the ones below:

Leave the Scene—Words spoken in anger are hardly ever well thought out. And once they've left our lips, we can't take them back. So if you find yourself really angry at someone, whether it's a spouse, a coworker, a child, or a family member, sometimes it's better just to walk away, give yourself time to cool off and re-center, and, if necessary, later return with a response that's coming from a place of reasoning instead of emotion. It's much better to say "I need a few minutes alone to get my thoughts together" than to say something you'll later regret.

Journal—If you often find yourself angry, try keeping a journal specifically to record your angry thoughts. Take note of what happened to make you mad, how you responded, how you feel about your response in retrospect, what thoughts were going through your mind, how your body responded, and what (if any) consequences came as a result of your response. After a week or so, or after about five or so entries, go back and read them. Look for patterns or triggers. This is an excellent way of managing your own emotions and taking responsibility for your reactions, as our reactions are the only thing we are capable of controlling.

Meditate—If this sounds like too foreign of a concept, try to just sit down and take some deep breaths instead, closing your eyes or not. When we're upset, our body responds as well. Our shoulders tense, our jaws clench, our legs tighten, and our breathing gets really shallow. Taking a deep breath sends a signal to your brain to relax. It takes your body out of fight or flight mode and re-centers your mind.

Take Five, Ten, or Twenty-Four—I've been using what I call the five-second tip technique for years. When someone says something offensive to you, don't say anything for five seconds. Your initial reaction might be to explode, go off, or get defensive, but if you wait five seconds to let yourself come back down from that first, immediate reaction, you'll most likely have a different response. Use those five seconds to use the "3 D" approach and consider, "Does what I have to say need to be said? Does it need to be said by me? Does it need to be said right now?" Your response, as a result, will be more rational instead of irrational.

Counting to ten also helps. Sometimes five seconds isn't sufficient. There is a reason we tell children to go count to ten in a corner, because it allows an irrational state of mind to come back down to a rational state of thinking. The same applies for a twenty-four-hour delay. Wait twenty-four hours, and you will see that usually the next day your anger will have settled after you've had time to think about it. You will be more calm, cool, and collected.

Talk About It—Process it with someone else. Reach out to someone you love and trust or who you are comfortable with to talk about it. As the AA saying goes, "You are only as sick as your secrets," and you don't want to continue harboring resentment toward someone who has probably forgotten about you and moved on with their life. You don't want to continue to be bitter and miserable for the rest of your life. Talk to someone, as they might very well offer insight or a more productive perspective on the matter.

Talking about your anger instead of just reacting is also important when disciplining children. When parents yell at their children, it makes the child feel like they're not loved because their parent is screaming, yelling, or even cursing at them. Now, the parent is really going off because of what the child did, but the child doesn't see it that way because the parent is being aggressive. So what do you, as the parent, do in that situation? When you get upset and you feel like you are getting ready to explode, you should back up, breathe, and be quiet; count to ten; or walk away. When you go to talk to that child, then, you are now addressing the behavior. You are not addressing the person—and that is what we have to learn to do in general. We have to learn to guide our anger in another direction, however long it takes, then come back and address the behavior. When you talk to the person, therefore, you will more clearly speak on the behavior, separating the emotion from the relationship.

Analyze Its True Cause—When we feel like our basic needs are violated—when we feel like someone or something is violating our family, our joy, our peace, our love, our security, our enjoyment, our everything—that is when we respond in anger. In addition to coping with our anger when it arises, it's important to get to the root of the issue that's causing the anger and then to release it. Anger is kind of like walking around with a rock in a bag on your shoulder. You keep adding one rock at a time, and before you know it, you can't even walk anymore because the bag is so heavy. Those rocks might be old situations of being disrespected, mistreated, abused, cussed out, stolen from, or lied to. And if you don't start taking those rocks out of your bag, they will continue to affect you as move forward.

Remember, anger is not, at heart, about the situation. Anger is your response to your belief about the situation. We can't control people, and things happen every day, but it is your belief about what has happened which causes you to respond. So if something happens, you have to say to yourself, "Okay, 5 percent of this emotion has to do with this particular situation. Ninety-five percent, though, is an unresolved issue from my past."

If you are angry with yourself, that same philosophy still applies. You need to peel the layers back.

As if you are going to cook, peel the layers of that onion back one at a time to discover the root of your anger. With each peeled layer, hold the onion—the situation—up to the light. In doing so, you'll realize that your anger most likely wasn't even about the situation. It was about that 95 percent of your belief about the situation, about what happened to you back in the day that let you down.

Ever met someone who reminded you of something or someone from your past? Or maybe you could never pinpoint why you never liked a certain person, despite the fact that they never did anything to you personally. It was the way they looked, the way they walked, their skin tone, their fingernails, the way they talked, the way they smelled. You didn't really care for the person and, unintentionally, may have mistreated the person. It really wasn't about the person, however. It was about your belief system. Perhaps someone in the past abused or mistreated you, and the certain person had a trait that resembled that person from the past, so you were transferring your past issues and anger onto the new person.

Practice Forgiveness—People who have been hurt have the right to be angry and resentful. These are normal reactions and emotions when feeling the disappointment and subsequent disempowerment that can come from being disrespected, betrayed, or abused. If not managed, however, anger can disrupt your health and your relationships, and therefore your happiness.

Anger isn't comfortable, nor is it easy to address. Yet it needs to be acknowledged and processed if you're to ever move on and begin enjoying life freely, and practicing forgiveness is an integral part of that process. Before you can truly forgive (and not just say you have), you have to acknowledge that you're angry, that you were hurt, and, if applicable, that you carry desires of revenge and ill-will toward those who hurt you. Acknowledging your offender's humanity also helps. This is called compassion, finding common ground, and realizing that we're all doing the best we can, given the experiences life has presented us.

Sometimes (read: most times), the offender is you. That's why self-forgiveness is of utmost importance. It's critical to the healing process. In forgiving yourself, you have to realize and accept your humanness. You're bound to make mistakes, to overlook what you believe you should've seen coming. Forgiving yourself also involves releasing thoughts of how things should be or would be and seeing them for what they are through a lens of compassion. You can be simultaneously ambitious in changing your reality and compassionate in accepting it for what it is today.

I'm not saying that anger is wrong. It's not. It's a natural reaction that teaches us a lot about ourselves and motivates us to make necessary changes in our personal lives and in the world. For centuries, people have marched into the streets and into the polls, demanding change—not because they were content, but because they were angry. Anger is only wrong when you exhibit a harmful behavior as a result of it. It is okay to get angry; it is how you carry yourself in anger that makes the difference. That it is why it is so important to use these coping skills. Practice, practice, practice.

And remember: The only person you can control is yourself. You cannot control other people. No matter how many times you try to help someone else, they might not be ready to change. So if that person responds to you in a very aggressive manner, you have to remember that you are the one learning the skills. It's up to you to express your anger in a healthy way and not let yourself be trapped by it.

Chapter 2
Rigid Belief Systems

In chapter 1, I mentioned "belief systems" a good bit, and how they are a major influence in our emotions and behaviors. This chapter explores those belief systems in depth, analyzing where they come from, how they affect our relationships, and how we should manage them. Everyone sees the world differently. My perception is my reality, and your perception is your reality. It is not my job to get you to see reality how I see it or convert you to my way of thinking, or vice versa. But where do our belief systems originate? We acquire our core beliefs through life experiences, especially during childhood, and they're established through our five senses—what we see, hear, taste, touch, and smell. We learn them through our parents, caregivers, teachers, and other influencers.

Conflict arises when our core belief system is violated or challenged. If I have a strong belief and you have a strong belief, and you violate my belief, now we have conflict. In matters of disagreement, we typically have one goal, to be understood and validated. When you have a rigid belief, however, you're not receptive to the viewpoints of other people. It's either your way or no way. Within this mindset, you're planning everyone else's life. You find yourself making plans for someone else before he or she has had an opportunity to opt out. You're probably a big fan of having things go the way you want them to go. If someone doesn't conform to your system, that's when the conflict leads to miscommunication and anger.

Conflict arises when there's a lack of empathy. Sympathy, a term we're most familiar with, is when I feel sorry for you from the outside looking in. Empathy, on the other hand, is me trying to see things how you see things. Now, that doesn't necessarily mean that we will come to see things in the same way; we may have to agree to disagree. If I'm being empathetic, that doesn't necessarily mean I agree with you, but it does mean I'm getting a chance to see things from your perspective. But to do so, I have to be open to seeing where you're coming from. Once I do that, I can weigh the pros and cons and, if necessary, go back and challenge what I believe about the subject or situation.

Your personal belief system can work for you or it can work against you. When it works against you, it's going to affect your relationships, your attitude, and your general sense of happiness and fulfillment. But there are ways to help you keep your belief systems in check.

Opening Up to Someone Else's Viewpoints

There was a man whose wife always cut off the end of the ham before cooking it. He'd ask her, "Why do you keep cutting off the end of the ham?" She'd say, "Because my mama did it." So one day he went to her mother and asked, "Why did you teach your daughter to cut off the end of the ham?" She responded, "I don't know. My mama did it." So he went to the grandmother and asked, "Why did you teach your daughter to teach my wife to cut off the end of the ham?" And she said, "Well, I went to the store and bought a ham one day. I brought it home and the pan was too small, so I cut off the end of the ham so it'd fit in the pan." The man's wife was cutting off the end of the ham for no reason, not knowing why she was doing it. She was just doing what she was taught.

How many of us have a belief system that we adhere to because that's what we were taught and that's all we know? We come into the world relating everything around us to our own experiences. We are our own point of reference. One of a toddler's favorite words is "mine!" If a child is thirsty, even if the parents are busy and cannot immediately help them, the child is only concerned about "cup" and will repeat this word (or one like it), getting louder and louder until their needs are met. As we grow, however, we learn the importance of stepping outside of our ego to see things from others' perspectives.

By opening ourselves to another person's viewpoints, we broaden our own. We become aware of not only our actions, but the repercussions of those actions as well. Understanding action and consequence fortifies our sense of ownership and personal responsibility, as well as teaches us to stop assuming and to consider as many sides of a situation as we can before reaching a conclusion. You have to get to the root of why you believe what you believe and be willing to challenge your belief systems and be empathetic to the viewpoints of other people. Here are a few proven methods for effectively opening up to someone else's viewpoints:

Active Listening—Active listening is a tool that is used to resolve conflicts and improve communication overall. It requires the listener to fully concentrate and to seek to understand. Fully concentrating means to really tune in to what the person is telling you. While they're talking, you aren't thinking of what to say next. You aren't being defensive or trying to further clarify your point. You aren't interrupting, and you surely aren't using any electronic devices while they're speaking. Instead, you are making eye contact and giving them your undivided attention. This also includes using positive gestures and being aware of your body language (folded arms, for instance, aren't very welcoming).

Once they've finished talking, it's your turn to seek to understand, to make sure you understand what they said. You should first acknowledge and validate their point of view. Do this by asking nonjudgmental questions. Get to know them. Feel them out. See where they're coming from. Responses that can help with this are: "Okay, so what you're saying is . . ." or, "Can you expand on this a little bit more?" Reflect on what's been said by paraphrasing. Phrases like "What I'm hearing is . . ." and "Sounds like you are saying . . ." are great ways to reflect back, further engage in their world, and see things the way they do. Then, once it's time for you to express how you feel, understand that it's still not about you. You're instead empathizing with that person and experiencing what they're feeling.

Be Vulnerable—Too many conversations stay in emotional safe zones. We fear vulnerability because we're afraid of what others may perceive about us. Many people shy away from vulnerability because they associate it with being emotional. The two aren't the same, however. Being vulnerable isn't about telling your deepest secrets. It's about being open and honest. To help you out, one way to approach being vulnerable is to first try to think of a time you were in a similar situation to the one that the speaker is referencing. Remember what you felt like in that situation, then express that feeling to the other speaker and share what you learned through the process.

When opening yourself up to someone else's viewpoints, don't assume you know the final answer. Jumping too soon to a conclusion can be an indication of a prejudice. You're pre-judging the situation before the facts. So many relationships fail because people are being prejudiced. Don't try to empathize before you truly understand the situation.

Roadmap to Victory

The first thing you have to do is realize that you have a rigid belief in the first place. That's number one, acknowledging that you are stuck in a belief system. Then you have to stumble a bit. It's called empathy; not sympathy, but empathy. Sympathy is when you feel sorry for somebody, but empathy is when you actually realize that you need to try to see it from someone else's perspective. Remember, you're not trying to get them to conform to your belief. It's important to catch yourself if you start to do that, because it's easy to slip into that mindset.

We've been conditioned to see a disagreement like a tug-of-war: each person is trying to pull the other person over. That's not the case at all, however. Your goal is to make your stance clear and understood, and then you need to listen to and empathize with the person you're disagreeing with so that you can see the way they feel about things. An effective affirmation to remember and repeat is: My perception is my reality. Your perception is your reality.

We don't have to see things alike. Everybody views the world differently through our individual senses—what we hear, see, taste, touch, feel, and smell. So if I'm going to overcome my rigid belief when someone does something offensive to me, I have to try to see it from their perspective. If I see it from their perspective, it's going to help me to understand them better. If someone brings something to me, I've got to listen to their perspective, see it from their perspective, and then I've got to be able to acknowledge that my belief might not be right, and that perhaps I need to challenge that belief.

Chapter 3:
Miscommunication

Here is the cycle of communication: You have the sender and you have the receiver. The sender sends a message to the receiver, then the receiver becomes the new sender and sends feedback back to the original sender, acknowledging the message, and the cycle repeats. You have conversations every day, whether internally with your thoughts or externally. You are talking to yourself or talking to someone else all day long.

Communication is like tennis. You go back and forth, back and forth, right? It is a smooth transition. Sometimes communication is not that way, though. Sometimes communication occurs where one person strikes the ball and the other person can't return the strike. This might be because the message was aimed somewhere that the other person couldn't respond, or because the message was sent in a way that made it difficult to receive or return. The way messages are sent is often determined by the kind of relationship the people who are communicating have with each other.

There are different ways we can communicate or relay a message to someone; these include communicating aggressively, passively, passive-aggressively, or assertively.

Aggressive

Aggressive communication is seen in somebody who can be verbally aggressive, verbally abusive, or physically abusive, or in somebody who is dominant. They are condescending, they talk down to you, and they belittle you; they feel like they are in control over you. Where does that come from, that mindset? It can come from a lot of things.

Maybe someone was aggressive toward them as they were growing up, which made them copy that as their method of communication. Maybe they were abused physically, verbally, or sexually, which caused aggression to come out in everything they do. Another possibility is that the aggressive communicator had someone under their care when growing up due to parental absence. Oftentimes a custodial parent may work multiple jobs to financially provide for the family, depending on the eldest child to oversee the household. They were young, maybe eight or ten years old, and they had siblings who were younger than them. They had to take care of those siblings, not by choice, but rather by circumstances, so the siblings kind of answered to them. In turn, this gave the aggressive communicator the mindset of "I depend on you to depend on me, so I can talk to you any kind of way, because without me, you will not be successful." So when someone doesn't do what that person says, they get very aggressive.

Passive

Someone who is passive, on the other hand, was most likely abandoned, neglected, deprived of validation, or faced with disapproval at a young age. Their parent might've left them physically and/or emotionally, leaving a hole, a void in their heart. As a result, they became excessively dependent and needed to fill that gap, whether that be with drugs, sexual relations, unhealthy relationships, gangs, overeating, overspending, gambling, or accumulating stuff. A passive person has the mindset of "I need you," which complements the aggressive person's mindset of "I need you to need me." The passive person says "I depend on you;" the aggressive person says "I depend on you to depend on me."

More harmful, the aggressive person has the mindset of "I matter and you don't," and the passive person has the mindset of "I don't matter and you do." Passivity is very indirect and non-confrontational. Someone exhibiting it will let the aggressor trample over them, treat them like a doormat, and won't say anything. On the inside, they are really angry, but you will rarely see it on the outside. The passive person allows the aggressive person to dominate them because they don't want to experience being abandoned again. They were already left as a child and they know what that felt like, so they say to themselves, "I never want that to happen to me again." Inside it is killing them, that this person is abusive to them, mistreats them, and so forth, but they don't want to get left again, so a lot of times they stay in these relationships to avoid having to restart their life. Frequently, the passive person then goes into what we call passive aggression.

Passive-Aggressive

Passive-aggressive communication says, "I don't matter and neither do you. Neither one of us matters." A passive-aggressive person may be smiling on the outside like everything is all good, but underneath the surface, they are demonstrating aggressive anger. It'll show up as, for instance, losing your job just to disrupt the financial balance in the house, making a lot of noise while your partner is sleeping, leaving the bath water on all night, coming home late at night, forgetting to clean the toilet before company arrives, etc. You're doing everything except communicating what's wrong. This type of communication can manifest itself at very specific times, ones where it is most disruptive.

Assertive

Then you have assertive communication. Assertive communication is a useful communication tool. It is the ability to verbalize positive and negative ideas and feelings in an honest and direct way. This communication style helps one to articulate their message constructively, confronting and finding a mutually satisfying solution where conflict exists. Some advantages to assertive communication are that it helps us to reduce anxiety, make decisions and free choices in life, increase self-esteem, develop mutual respect with others, feel good about ourselves, achieve our goals, express positive and negative thoughts, and minimize hurting other people. Keep in mind, others can perceive sudden assertiveness as an act of aggression. Some characteristics of assertive communication are: eye contact; respectful body posture, body language, gestures, voice level, and content; and being aware of where and when you choose to comment. "I" statements are very important when communicating assertively. "I" statements display ownership, directness, and honesty, and contribute to improved relationships. For example, instead of saying, "You always come home late," you might say, "I feel frustrated when you come home late; it puts a strain on me getting the kids ready for bed."

If the sender of a message is not skilled in communicating, they may inadvertently send the wrong type of message or have its meaning interpreted in a way that wasn't intended. Suppose the sender lacks rapport with the receiver, for example, or the receiver disrespected them or violated their belief system before the sender sends the message. Similarly, if the receiver doesn't like the sender, sometimes no matter what the sender says the receiver is not receptive and the attempt at communication can escalate to aggression.

The receiver's job in communication is to decode the message of the sender. When you decode a message, that means you understand the intended message. Fifty-five percent of the way you communicate is body language, 38 percent is tone of voice, and 7 percent is the actual words that you say. So when the sender sends a message to you, as the receiver, you have to decode the words, the tone, and the body language of the sender.

When you encode a message as a sender, you have to make sure that you have thought all of that through. Any one of the three components of a message, body language, tonality, and words, can distort the intended message. When getting ready to send a message while thinking irrationally, you might consider waiting a few hours to calm down. You have to take an inventory and ask yourself, what is my intended outcome with this message? You want to make sure that your body language is appropriate, you want to make sure that your tone of voice is appropriate, and you want to make sure that the words you say are used in an assertive manner by saying "I" instead of "you." Say "I feel this way," not "You made me feel this way."

When you send a message, you are encoding it and sending the message over. Then, the other person has to decode the message, decode what you have just said—and they'll start from the way you sent the message. So if you sent the message in a disrespectful manner, the person may not decode the message properly and may respond in an equally disrespectful manner.

You can't control how the person receives it; you can only control how you send it. If you don't feel like your body language is going to be appropriate when you send a message, you should wait until you get to a place where you can be calm, cool, and collected before you send that message.

The receiver needs to do what is called active listening, which we talked about in Chapter 2. A lot of the time, when people send messages to us, as soon as we hear something that we don't like, we get defensive and say things like "I don't mean to cut you off, but . . ." We get rude. As receivers, we have to learn to become trained listeners.

Don't focus on the person; instead, listen to the message. You have to separate your preconceptions about the person who is saying it from the message itself and listen to what they are saying. The job of the receiver is to decode what the person is saying. "What I hear you saying is this . . ." Now, when you hear what a person tells you as a receiver and you don't feel you can decode it properly, you don't need to respond right away. You can take some time to figure out what that person is saying. A lot of times, when we receive a message, we want to start talking about how we feel and what we think should happen right away, instead of taking the time to properly decode it.

As the sender of a message, I just want to know that you hear what I had to say, not necessarily that you are agreeing or not agreeing; I just want to know that you hear me. So as the receiver, your job is to decode it. You can use statements such as, "so what I hear you saying is this, is that correct? Am I hearing you correctly?" You are letting that person know that you hear them. When you encode that back to them, guess what they have to do? They have to decode what you just said.

So that is the cycle; whatever the way you encode a message, that is the way they are going to decode it. You have to send out an encode to receive a decode; the receiver sends an encode back to the sender and the sender has to decode what the receiver just said. Both just want to be heard.

We all communicate with words today. But while there was a time when you could talk to somebody face-to-face, shake hands with the person, and have the situation taken care of and done with, today there are so many different ways to communicate. You have text messaging, phone calling, and social media. The face of communication is changing. Consequently, how we deal with conflict is changing as well.

One thing that can be helpful when communicating in a tense situation is to know what type of arguer you and/or your opponent are. If you can identify what you're dealing with, you can come up with strategies to get around any hurdles and still effectively communicate. Here are nine types of arguers:

The Screamer

The screamer is an explosive type personality. When they get into a confrontation, instead of reacting calmly or rationally, they scream, yell, and holler. They are belittling, condescending, demeaning, and argumentative. It may be what they saw growing up, from their parents, coach, or other authority figure.

This type of arguer may originate with someone who, when growing up, could never do anything right and always used to have people scream at them. They then develop a mindset that when anyone doesn't do something right, you scream at them. Remember, in communication, the whole point is that you want to be heard. You want others to hear what you are saying. A screamer is very similar to someone who exhibits explosive anger—they scream, then they come back down and feel bad. They got that high that they needed when they screamed.

The Slammer

This type of arguer will slam doors, pots and pans, shoes, etc. That is the way they get their anger out. When they communicate by slamming and breaking things, it makes them feel empowered and dominant, in charge. That bully mindset of "how dare you talk to me like that" is common in the slammer.

The Follower

The follower is a person who follows the person they are arguing with all through the house, or wherever they are. They want to be heard, and if someone walks away from them, they are going to follow that person until they get out what they need to say.

The Thrower

This is someone who is always throwing something. They are similar to the slammer, but instead of just making noise and breaking things, they're throwing objects at people.

The Historian

The historian is the person who knows they have been apologized to exactly 332 times and have kept the record of everything the other person has done. They can state the time, the position of the sun, the phase of the moon, and the temperature that day and can recall every facet of wrongdoing. They may be smiling and saying "I forgive you," but they record everything and bring it up at the most opportune time to try to score a point with that person; that is a historian. The historian is not gender specific. Historians are very common, because it's tempting to take notes and store up points for future conflicts.

The Curser

Profane language is this person's way of communicating. They are very condescending and love using profanity, not thinking about the connotation of their words. Their way of speaking is through insulting, belittling, or demeaning somebody.

The Silencer

Silent communication says, "I am not going to speak to you, but I am also not going to say nothing to you. I am going to let you guess all of what I am thinking." A lot of times, a silencer, somebody who loves silent treatment, will try to get a response out of you, will try to get you to go off. Sometimes the silent treatment person is trying to leave the relationship, and they feel that if they can stay silent and get you to go off and do something crazy in an explosive manner, that would justify their making the decision to leave. They will go for days and not say anything to you, making you have to guess at whatever you have done.

The Winner

The winner is not going to stop until they win the argument. They have to have the last word. No matter how the conversation concludes, they ensure you hear them last.

The Sniper

The sniper is the person who knows how to hit you right where it hurts. Nobody can hurt you like this person; only people you've had the most intimate relationships with can aim their barbs so accurately. They know how to say just one thing to you that will get you all explosive, make you start cursing, screaming, and yelling. We all have somebody that can do that to us—but the real question is, who do *you* do that to? Everyone has somebody who they can rile up at any time.

You can be all of these types of arguers at different points in your life or relationships. Giving the silent treatment, throwing things, yelling, following, having to have the last word . . . You can relate to all these behaviors. The objective of identifying all these types of arguers is not to attach yourself to any particular type; rather, it's to be able to see yourself in them as a means of acknowledgement, so that you can begin moving in the direction of overcoming your limitations and communicating more effectively.

Don't be fooled by technology; these behaviors can show up in texting and emailing as well. When we don't want to use voice tone, body language, and eye contact to communicate, electronic communication often supersedes verbal communication. But you can still tell what type of communicator someone is by their quantitative words in their text message or email. The "ten second responders" demonstrate quantity verses quality, for instance, and can respond almost immediately to a situation with a whole paragraph. They don't even care about the grammatical errors. They "go off," texting every thought that enters their mind. They appear dramatic and erratic. So even in text messaging, you can tell the type of person someone is.

Roadmap to Victory

We've all had weak moments in our lives when our attempts at communication failed us. We responded in ways we later regretted or found embarrassing. Maybe someone wronged us according to our belief system, a situation didn't go our way, we were disappointed, we were tired, we were overstimulated, or we were just plain fed up, and as a result, we didn't behave rationally.

It's impossible to always communicate perfectly. It's how we handle the situation when we miscommunicate that matters. Below are the stages of improving communication. You might not necessarily go through them in this order, and you might not necessarily spend equal amounts of time in each stage. You could, for instance, zoom to Stage 3 and stay there for years. The goal, however, is commitment and consistency, to break the cycle that's causing dysfunction in your relationship with yourself and those around you. Be patient with yourself, though. That's important.

Stage 1: Pre-Contemplation

There's nothing wrong with me. I don't need help; I'm okay with my current life, despite the problems that arise from miscommunication.

Stage 2: Contemplation

I see where I want to go, but I don't know how I am going to get there. I see the behavior I am trying to obtain, but I don't know how to obtain it, so I am stuck. I don't know how to make it happen.

Stage 3: Preparation

I'm preparing for change by consulting with professionals and researching solutions. However, I'm stumbling when it comes to implementing those solutions.

Stage 4: Action

I am not changed, but I am changing. I was stuck, I was stumbling, but now I am standing. I am actually using coping skills and communication skills now: body language, voice tone, verbal cues, and nonverbal cues.

Stage 5: Maintenance

I have now changed my communication pattern to assertiveness, and continue to maintain the new behavior.

Chapter 4
Codependency

Relationships are an innate part of life. They're with us from the day we're born until the day we leave this earth. As we grow and mature, we expand our social circles beyond our immediate families into friendships, intimate relationships, parenthood, and more. The relationships that you want—whether with your mother, child, or spouse—are based on pillars such as respect, trust, support, honesty, good communication, and separate identities. Those are healthy relationships.

A common example of an unhealthy relationship, however, is one that involves dependency. I'm not talking about a child being dependent on their parent to provide for them. I'm talking about excessive dependency in the sense of relying on someone else (or something else) for the existence of your self-worth. For example, it's needing to spend a certain amount of money on your clothes to feel worthy, or needing to be in a relationship to feel good about yourself, to have your emotional needs met.

Then you have what's called codependency, when two dependent people are addicted to depending on one another. A codependent relationship is one-sided, with Partner A needing Partner B to need them.

Because Partner B is not very confident on their own, they look to Partner A to fill a void, to rescue them. Partner A is most likely addicted to relationships, jumping from one to another, and can be very manipulative and jealous. As a result, Partner B has hardly any time or energy to fulfill their own needs, because they are constantly worried about how Partner A feels and what Partner A needs. While it may sound like codependency is limited to romantic relationships, it also shows up in parenting and friendships.

You might wonder what makes Partner B stick around. In short, it's because Partner B also needs Partner A; they need one another (and for very unhealthy reasons). Let's call Partner A the rescuer and Partner B the rescued. Alternate terminology could be the saved and the savior, but we'll used the rescuer and the rescued here.

The rescuer is saying to the rescued, "I depend on you to depend on me." The rescued is saying, "I need you, because growing up I didn't have anyone." Opposites attract, right? So you have two people coming together in an unhealthy relationship. Once together, manipulation is often present, particularly in cases where the rescuer has more money or formal education than the rescued.

The person who needs to be rescued was possibly abandoned at a very young age. Maybe one of their parents walked out or departed their life suddenly. There's an emotional void that needs to be filled, so some turn to drugs, alcohol, gangs, promiscuous relationships, or gambling. They're trying to be validated, rescued. On the other hand, the rescuer was possibly at a very young age elevated to parental status or ultra-responsibility. Usually, their parent excessively depended on them to meet their own personal needs, causing them to raise their siblings and provide food, clothing, and shelter. Rescuers can exhibit aggressive, controlling behaviors because people depend on them to function.

Another function of a codependent relationship is that it allows one party to continue their addictive and/or underachieving behavior. If that person were single, they would have to face themselves. But because they're in a relationship that doesn't challenge them to do more, they don't. Codependency is a relationship addiction; you need it to function. As with all addictions, it gives us something else to focus on besides ourselves.

Relationships provide us with the powerful opportunity to see ourselves and see areas in our own lives where we need to grow. With each conflict, we learn more about our partners and more about ourselves. We see where our ego is taking over, and we learn to manage it. Relationships are excellent mirrors—but only when we allow them to be. Codependency does not allow that self-reflection. Instead of feeling like fresh air, codependent relationships leave you feeling trapped.

Do you feel trapped in your relationship? Do you spend all of your energy trying to meet all of your partner's needs? Does your existence involve making sacrifices to please your significant other? Do you struggle with saying no when you partner insists on spending time together? Do you shield your partner's legal, drug, or alcohol issues? Are you paranoid or constantly worried about how people view you? Are you the only one in the relationship making sacrifices? Do you keep quiet to avoid arguments? Does your relationship feel less like a 50/50 and more like a 90/10? Any of these could be a classic sign of codependency.

Other signs of codependency include low self-esteem and people-pleasing behavior. When you have low self-esteem, you feel you aren't good enough, so you constantly compare yourself to others. You see everything that they have and that you don't. It could be physical traits or material objects. You're constantly looking at what's wrong with you. People pleasers have a hard time saying no because they fear abandonment. They would rather say yes, even though they should really be saying no, because they feel they don't have a choice; their boundary lines are blurry (if present at all).

The symptoms of codependency have a domino effect. As a result of lacking boundaries, a codependent person reacts to everything. They're notorious for taking things personally and being defensive. It's hard to just shrug something off as the other person's opinion, because they already feel insecure about the stability of the relationship and the security within themselves. Codependents also tend to be very controlling and bossy, constantly telling other people what they should or shouldn't do. This makes them feel safe and secure. That bossiness is a sign of not being able to effectively and respectfully communicate. They have trouble articulating their thoughts and feelings for a couple of reasons: 1) they aren't aware of them, and 2) they refuse to own their truth. This all comes down to fear, though. They're afraid to be alone, afraid of running their partner off. So they obsessively think about and talk about the relationship.

Another sign of codependency is persistent painful emotions. That's not to say that healthy relationships are always full of smiles and sunshine, because they aren't. But they aren't consumed with stress, jealousy, anxiety, and judgment, whereas codependent relationships are. In codependent relationships, the rescuer often sabotages the rescued's ability to do better for themselves. When the rescued goes and gets an education or coping skills or therapy, the rescuer cannot handle that, because now the rescuer feels threatened that their partner won't depend on them anymore. If they're not depended on, then the rescuer won't be able to manipulate the rescued anymore and the (im) balance in the home is ruined.

Roadmap to Victory

If you're the rescuer, you have to learn to depend on yourself. Ask yourself: why do you need to be depended on? Get to the root of it. Dig through your childhood, teenage, and early adulthood years. If no one depended on you for anything, how would that make you feel? While your immediate reaction might be to say "relieved," dig a little deeper and you might find "lonely" or even "worthless." And while neither of these are true about you, only you can convince yourself of that.

If, on the other hand, you are the rescued, you have to learn to start becoming independent and making decisions for yourself. Whether you go to counseling, go to church, or start reading self-help books, you need to find a place where you have positive affirmations to build yourself up. Again, most people who need to be rescued don't have high self-esteem. They don't believe in themselves and might be depressed.

The opposite of codependency is interdependence, which is healthy and balanced dependence. Interdependence requires two people capable of autonomy, who have the ability to function on their own. People in interdependent relationships take responsibility for their own actions. When people exhibit high self-esteem, they don't have to control another person to feel validated. An interdependent couple acknowledges one another's differences and belief systems. The key is to get to an interdependent relationship where it's healthy for both. If you're trying to (or need to) leave the relationship, the key is to become independent. But if you're trying to stay, then interdependency is the desired outcome.

Chapter 5
The Masks We Wear

The masks we wear are what people display in public. When people view the external you, what do they see? Is it your looks? Is it your body language? Is it your character? Is your character situational? Are you authentic, or are you fabricated? You can change your mask so often, so habitually, that it becomes routine and you don't even realize you're doing it, or even that you're wearing one. The question is: Does the external (known) you, which is open to the public, reflect the internal (hidden) you, which defines your true character? If a poll was taken about your residential character, your employment character, your religious character, your rational character, your irrational character, your social character, what would the results be? What would people say? How would it line up to the man or woman in the mirror?

Situations, thoughts, feelings, and behaviors are implanted into the mind at a young age. If you were not approved of or acknowledged as a child, or if you were abandoned, then you may wear different masks, depending on which crowd you're seeking acceptance from. Parents also may teach kids to wear masks indirectly. Kids may see their parents behave one way at home and another at church or around their friends. We model what we see growing up. Our homes are factories, our first schools, and where we learn behaviors and social norms.

School reinforces those behaviors. Everyone, from our teachers to our peers, teaches us the social value of wearing masks. We're told that code-switching is the key to success. The way you talk at home isn't the way you talk in your essay or at your interview. The way you dress around your friends may not be acceptable in a corporate board meeting.

People that we're acquainted with as children can teach us about masks. For instance, seeing your church leaders in one light, then learning how they behave behind closed doors, teaches us about masks. While it can initially be a shocking revelation, that knowledge can eventually validate a future choice that you have to make when it comes to showing up as one person for one group of people and as another person for another group of people.

Masks are not always harmful. The key is conscious awareness, asking yourself how the mask interferes—or shows up—in your daily life. Are you able to realize that you're wearing a mask, and which one it is? We can wear them so routinely that we become unaware of them; they become second nature. Possibly, too, we no longer notice our masks because we've been wearing them since childhood to fit in. We all want to be validated. We all want to matter to people. We want people to accept us. So, depending on the environment, we'll wear a certain mask in order to be accepted by that person or group of people.

There are different types of masks that people wear. Some of them include:

- **The Energy Drink Mask:** You're pretending to be full of energy, that you have it all together. You flash disingenuous smiles to make it appear that you are competent in what you're doing.

- **The Muscle Mask:** You're pretending to be strong, unstoppable, relentless, unmoved, and impenetrable, while on the inside, it's the exact opposite.

- **The Doctoral Mask:** You appear intelligent, unique, talented, and ambitious.

- **The Gold-Plated Mask:** You appear wealthy to fit in socially, when really you're struggling to make the minimum credit card payment.

- **The Good Person Mask:** You want to be liked. You're a people pleaser. You never, or rarely, say no, so that you can come across as that good person.

Let's look at the role of masks in intimate relationships. When the honeymoon phase fades and the honey drips off the moon, we often have to be careful, because the love we once had for our spouse can become a mask that's concealing unhappiness and resentment. Love can become mistaken for responsibility. One can secretly fall out of love but continue their role and responsibility in the relationship because of the mask that they wear. Within a relationship, a mask can be worn to cover several different things—unhappiness (my mate no longer excites me or brings me joy), loneliness (I feel isolated and alone), fear (what would I do if my mate was no longer present due to death or divorce?), or resentment (would we have gotten married if she hadn't gotten pregnant?).

In the church, we wear masks as well. If you grew up in the church, you may find that you're only going out of obligation; without some kind of spiritual research of your own, what could appear as active or faithful worship to God or your Higher Power could be a mask, covering up a vain worship. Masks are also worn in church to cover up doubt. Your faith is wavering, your spirit is low, you're in doubt, but you don't want to reveal that, not even to yourself. We can also easily get stuck in private struggles, in our weaknesses (substance abuse, pornography, gambling, etc.), and we wear masks to cover those up.

In the workplace, we frequently wear a mask when we go to work. A lot of employees are not satisfied with their jobs; we wear masks to appear satisfied, but we're really not. We don't want to be there, but we can't show that, because we need to keep our job to pay our bills. So we suffer through discontentment and stagnation. Masks can also be used to cover up racism, sexism, and more. Some people have trouble setting aside their personal feelings of hate in a particular environment. There's a lot of jealousy and envy in the workplace, too. Why was she promoted, when I wasn't? Why did he get this raise instead of me? Why did they get the job and not me? You have feelings of inadequacy—am I good at what I do? So you wear a mask because you don't want people to see how you're really feeling on the inside. You're stuck inside of this façade, while internally you're boiling over.

Roadmap to Victory

We wear these masks to feel accepted. In certain cases, they can lead to an approval addiction. You can't help but wonder, if the real you were to come out, would you still be accepted?

There's an old saying: "to thine own self be true." If you're not going to be true to yourself, then you're not going to be true to other people. Whatever it is that you don't like about yourself is what you need to address so that you can be you wherever you go. Below are three steps to help you do just that:

Step 1: Acknowledge the fact that you're pretending. Until then, you're going to continue to unconsciously and consciously wear a mask wherever you go.

Step 2: Verbalize your desire to live as the authentic you. That's where the preparation comes in. You have to establish a plan. You have to take each social setting that you see yourself in, see the problem, and want to align all of your presentations of self into one being.

Step 3: Put it into action. Now that you've addressed your character defects, it's time to be yourself everywhere you go.

As adults, we have to be mindful of the double standard we teach children. If we're telling them that they have to speak one way at home and another way on the job, then we're instilling in them at a very young age that who they are at their core is not acceptable, that it's not good enough. We're telling them that their best bet is to hide who they really are behind a mask, as opposed to teaching them the correct way to speak and dress from the start.

This can be particularly relevant to persons of color. We're taught from a young age—at home, at school, at church—to change everything about ourselves, including the pitch of our voice and the curl in our hair, to gain access and acceptance. We're told that no matter how much you love lime green suits and gator shoes, you had better not wear them anywhere near Corporate America. Furthermore, we're taught to work ten times harder than our peers to get and keep the same job as them.

It's Halloween for some people every day. But what's going to happen when that mask falls? What will happen to your job, your relationship, your leadership position? You can't wear a mask forever. It'll come off, and when it does, that's when someone will say, "I didn't know he was like that. I thought he was this way." It takes a lot of work to wear a mask. It's harder to wear one than it is to go without it.

Chapter 6:
Habits and Addictions

It's commonly believed that it takes twenty-one days to develop a habit or addiction. While this may be the case for some, or might be a general truth, it's certainly not the case for everyone. There are many factors at play that can help you understand addiction and the rate at which it develops, such as your environmental factors, biological factors, psychological factors, etc. We are unique individuals with unique life experiences, needs, wants, and struggles. The biggest factor in the development of habits and addictions, however, is your brain.

Before we get started, I'd like to make clear that while this chapter might mention substance use disorders, substance use is not the sole focus of the chapter. There are many habits and addictions that will be covered here.

While *habits* and *addictions* are very similar in meaning, they are not synonymous. A habit is the starting point, the beginning of the loop. It involves three things: a trigger, a routine, and a reward. After a long day (trigger), you come home and drink a glass of wine (routine) and it instantly calms your nerves (reward). Another example: Your alarm clock goes off at

7 am (trigger) and you choose to exercise before going to work (routine) because doing so gives you more energy and optimism (reward) throughout the day. Once you begin needing that glass of wine every day after work, though, then it's no longer a habit. It's a necessity, it's an addiction. The same can go for working out, too. Ever heard the saying, "Too much of anything is a bad thing"?

The first time someone uses a drug, he or she may begin immediately feeling the effects. Some people might try them and be averse to the change in heart rate or the feeling of being out of control, while others come to crave that feeling. Some drugs lead to a burst of euphoria. Others drugs classified as depressants, sedatives, or opioids, such as Xanax, Vicodin, and alcohol, depress our central nervous system, resulting in relaxation and reduced anxiety. Your brain reacts differently to each substance, with each drug affecting certain areas of the brain. Bryan Lewis Saunders, in 1995, conducted a (super dangerous, could've-been-fatal) experiment in which he took a different drug every day for thirty days. While high, he'd paint or draw a self-portrait. By looking at the various pieces of art, you can see how each had a different effect on his brain.

The same goes for addictions to sex, shopping, gambling, stealing, working out, eating, scrolling through social media, etc. They all trigger a unique pleasure point in the brain that makes us want more. Our likelihood of becoming addicted is influenced by who we were before the addiction and what we went through prior to becoming addicted. Again, it points back to childhood (and even before). For example, the levels of stress your mother endured while carrying you in her womb directly affected your brain as a fetus. The effect of this stress followed you into the world, influencing your long-term ability to manage your emotions. If never treated, this can lead to impulsivity and addiction.

If someone is missing something and they have a feeling of emptiness in their life (a common experience for teenagers and young adults), or they weren't given recognition growing up and now constantly need validation, they're more likely to form unhealthy attachments. A tendency to addiction can be hereditary, too. The woman whose mother was addicted to shopping is more likely to become addicted to acquiring material things as well. In my case, I was chronically angry, and had been for a very long time. Chronic anger, as we learned, promotes a sense of disempowerment, which only further fuels the anger and supports the use of drugs or alcohol. The substances act as a numbing agent and a distraction.

A lot of addictions start with curiosity. You see something, hear something, watch something on TV, and all of a sudden it's in your mind. Then, once you've experienced it for the first time, you have a sense of euphoria—whether it be eating a certain food, playing the slot machines, taking the drugs, having intercourse, etc. Once you've experienced what that moment will do for you, all of a sudden, when life hits you again, you crave that specific source of pleasure, that rush. By constantly indulging, you create the habit. Continue into the habit and eventually you crash. Once you've crashed in your life, you know what is going to make you feel a certain way again.

With my addiction to prescription painkillers, I started off with curiosity and landed at this behavior of making me feel relieved. Once I'd come back down, I'd be seeking that relief all over again. It'd become a habit. And once I was seeking that relief again, I'd be doing it at a much greater speed or rate, trying to get the same effect. In time, it'd grown from a habit to an addiction. Let's take gambling at the slot machine, for example. You win, you come back down, and you realize you need some money again. So back to the casino. Let's now say you don't get that big win on the first or second time. Now you're playing thirty or forty times, trying to get back the same hit, because you're trying to call back that experience of when you won.

That's the feel-good reward, and you start chasing it, just trying to feel better.

Once you're trapped in a habit or addiction, you pursue it despite the consequences. The behavior that you're portraying is more important to you than the consequences—whether those be losing your family, your career, your spiritual life, your social relations with people, your relationship with yourself, or your mental or physical wellbeing.

A few signs that you might be addicted:

- You lie about how much you actually do it when talking to someone about it, if you admit it at all.

- Those closest to you are constantly commenting on it or complaining about it.

- You can't cope without it, or if you can, you really struggle to.

- You're increasingly doing it more and more.

- It's crossed your mind several times that you need to cut back or stop.

- You say you're going to cut back or stop, only to fall right back into it.

- It's disrupting your relationships, performance, and/or finances.

Everyone has a habit of something—from harmless or beneficial ones like biting your nails, brushing your teeth every morning, speaking to those you encounter, and praying for people you know, to more serious ones like binging on pornography, over-consuming sweets, cutting people off while they're talking, and more. But if we don't stop to reflect on our actions and desires, those habits can quickly become addictions. And you can get so deep in an addiction or habit that you're doing it just to function as a normal person. You're no longer really doing it anymore to get a high or to feel a certain way, you're just trying to function.

Roadmap to Victory

Addiction is a sneaky disease. Keyword there is that it's a disease, like asthma is a disease of the lungs. Being addicted to something does not mean you're weak, inherently flawed, or a bad person. However, the reality of most diseases, including addiction, is that they require ongoing care to manage. It's a lifelong commitment that will not always be easy. For this reason, it's best to catch it before it becomes an addiction—before it becomes a habit, preferably. But things happen, and that's why I wrote this chapter, to help you untangle yourself from the trap of addiction.

While there are quite a few similarities among addicted individuals, each situation is unique, influenced by scores of biological, psychological, and social factors, such as age, gender, prior addictions, type of addiction, and family history. Because it's such a case-by-case basis, much like the grieving process, no two people's road to recovery will match. However, despite so many different influences and factors, most recovering addicts will experience similar stages on their path to freedom.

For the roadmap to victory in this case, I want to share some things to expect on the journey, as well as some common stages of addiction recovery.

What to expect:

- Getting sober is only the first step. Maintaining sobriety (or disengagement from that bad habit) is an entirely different battle.

- Emotions will run high. That's because it's a disease. Your brain is demanding more and you're not giving it, and your brain is throwing a mean tantrum that will show up in the form of anger, sadness, irritability, and more.

- You're going to have to pause or totally omit your old environments. If you have a habit of retail therapy, then it's not in your best interest to go window shopping with friends. Stay away from the stores for a while.

- You might lapse. You set a goal to limit your junk food to once a week. It ended up being three times last week, and this week, you gave up altogether. It's okay. Forgive yourself and get back on track.

Here are five common stages of addiction recovery:

1. You first have to realize that you're stuck. You're not considering change. Although you might still be engaging in the bad habit or addiction and haven't made any commitment or progress toward ending those behaviors, this first stage is crucial in paving the way for the rest of the process. One of the most important parts of this phase is the shift from having an awareness of the problem to actually acknowledging that action is needed. That's where step 2 comes in.

2. In this step, you're staring into the mirror and admitting to yourself, "Okay, I have an issue. I have a problem." You're acknowledging that change needs to happen within the next six months. Here's where the words *awareness* and *acknowledgement* show up again. You see that you have an issue, but now you have to try to figure out if you want to get out of the issue or stay stuck in that space. A lot of times we stay stuck in a habit, we stay stuck in an addiction, because

that's all we've known for so long. We don't know anything else and it becomes our norm. It becomes our comfortable element and we feel a fear of the unknown. And we have a fear of change (discussed more in the next chapter).

3. In this stage, you're stumbling. You're preparing for change within the next thirty days. You know where you want to go, but you don't know how to get there. This is the preparation stage. You're trying to get up, but you keep falling. It goes back to one of the points of what to expect: There's a good chance that you might lapse, but it's important to reconstruct your perspective. It's not failing. It's just part of the process. A lot of times, when people are stumbling and they fall, they get discouraged and they go back to that known space. They go back to that known way of living, because it's comfortable for them and they feel it doesn't make sense to keep putting forth the effort. It takes effort to change, so you move back and forth between the different stages, working to progress but sometimes falling back. The stumbling process can last a long time when you're dealing with a long-term chronic habit or chronic addiction, something that you've been dealing with for years. You can change, relapse, change, and relapse. That's why

I call it the stumbling phase. Because you get up, you fall down, you get up, you fall down, but the key is, when you fall down, you've got to learn from the lesson, so that when you get up you don't fall because of the same situation and the same reason.

4. This is what we call the standing phase. You're changing; you're in that six months period you set in step 2. The standing phase is action, and now, your actions are portraying your new behavior. You're actually making the changes, making behavioral changes. During the standing stage, you may begin educating yourself about addiction, your family history, your personal patterns, and the recovery process. You might reach out to others who've been down a similar path for advice, and you might also consider therapy or treatment in this stage.

5. Here's the maintenance stage, where you've completely turned your life over and you are maintaining this new behavior, this new habit, this new lifestyle that you have. You've changed. By the time you've reached this fifth stage, you've made great progress. Perhaps most importantly, you have learned that you'll need to continue to maintain it for the rest of your life

(it's a lifestyle after all) to guard against relapse. This will require mindfulness in your day-to-day, moment-by-moment thoughts and behaviors.

Chapter 7
Known and Unknown

A lot of times we get trapped in the known way of our daily operations; we've engaged in a certain lifestyle for so long that it becomes our known way of living. For example, a small fish in a fishbowl becomes familiar with its environment. But once that fish starts to get large, it starts to outgrow its surroundings. Once the fish transitions to a large tank, it once again has become the small fish and must readjust to its new environment.

There were these people that had a baby bear. They put the bear in a cage, and every day the bear would pace back and forth in that 4x4-foot cage. Someone suggested blindfolding the bear to see how it would affect his pacing. It didn't alter his course at all, however. He would automatically know when to turn around, even when he was in his blindfold. Eventually, that bear got big and they had to put him in a 12x12 cage, but that bear would do the same thing. He would only walk four feet then turn around. He wouldn't walk the full cage. That 4x4 cage was his norm, his comfort zone. That's what he knew. That was his way of life. It was unknown to him, being in that new cage. He brought that old cage mentality to the new cage.

A lot of times we remain trapped in our old environment and don't shift to our new environment because we have a fear of the unknown; we have a fear of our new surroundings. If I go to a new relationship, a new city, a new job, I can't take my old mentality with me. I have to be open-minded. It's a learning process for me all over again. Do I really want to leave my current situation and go start all over again? What if it doesn't work for me?

When people come to me fearing a new change in their life, I ask three questions. Number one: what are you holding on to? Let's take a person, for example, in a relationship they're trying to get out of and move on from. But it's difficult because they're holding on to the way it used to be when they first met their partner. Maybe you're holding on to how that job used to be when you first got hired. You're holding on to how your health used to be or how your housing situation used to be. Well, days have gone by, months have gone by, years have gone by, and it's not that way anymore. That person that you first met, they don't exist anymore. That job is different. It's different. Saying you want to move in a new direction while holding on to who or what that person or thing used to be is contradictory and non-progressive.

Number two: what will your future look like if nothing changes? People hold on to potential, what they hope a person or place can become. Maybe that person will become what I need and want in the future. You're holding on to that hope, you have that hope. Well, you know what? They may never become that person. So you look up, twenty years have gone by, and that person hasn't changed. That job hasn't changed. That situation hasn't changed, yet you're still trapped in it.

That leaves the third question: what do you see in the here and now? Do you like what you see now? Are you able to be content with the job you have now, the person you have now, your current health status? Because remember, that person that they used to be, they're gone. That person you want them to be, you don't know if they'll ever be that person. So you have to be in the here and now. Live your life in the here and now.

Fear of the unknown is fear of shifting to a new dimension. Wherever you are in life, you have to first acknowledge your fear. List your thoughts and fears on paper; get it out of your head. *You know what? I'm a little afraid to step out. What if they don't like me? What if it doesn't work? What if I get terminated from my job? What if this happens? What if that happens? What if it's the wrong move?* You have to acknowledge that you have fears: I'm stuck, I know what I want to do, but I don't know how to get there. At this point, you're stumbling, preparing, contrasting the pros and cons. What are the advantages of taking this risk? What are the disadvantages? The decision may be to transition to the unknown, but the decision has to be to deal with the here and now, first and foremost.

Keep in mind that a lot of people don't want to move from the known to the unknown because they fear losing status. This was the case with me for in transitioning out of one church and into another. I'd spent so much time and energy moving the one church in a particular direction, only to have to pick up and start over at another. That's intimidating. What if they didn't accept me and my vision? Say you're the supervisor on your job, for instance. You've climbed all the way to the top and you're now maxed out. That can be frustrating, not being able to climb any higher, but it's also comforting. Moving to another company might lessen your power/seniority a bit before you're able to advance, but are you willing to take a chance?

This is where adopting a new perspective comes in. Instead of seeing it as starting over from the bottom, what if you saw it as elevating to a new job? Anytime you elevate from the known to the unknown, it's not that you're going down, it's that you're moving to a new dimension. You're just having to start over and learn something all over again. And once you max that out, you're shifting to the very next level. It's like working out. You might start off using 50-pound weights, but if you want to see progress, you can't stay there. You have to increase the weights, get out of your comfort zone. That's how life is. Once you've maxed out something, it's time to shift to the next dimension. When you shift there, have an open mind, talk to people, and reach out.

Now here's the kicker: eventually the unknown becomes your known. When you have a new known, then you need to start pushing yourself to the next unknown. I read a meme on Facebook that stated, "It's crazy. Working on yourself never ends. You get better and then, boom. Now it's new things you gotta work on. You're just unlocking endless levels of growth." I couldn't agree more. And those new levels of growth might provoke yet another fear of the unknown, but you'll be more equipped this time, because you've done it before.

Sometimes in life, you have to go for it. You have to get out there and make it happen. However, you have to weigh the pros and cons. If it's going to hurt you, your family, or somebody else, then it's not a wise choice. You have to reevaluate if it's the right move for you. But always keep in mind that we only live one time. We don't get a do-over in life. You get one chance to live this life, and you want to push for greatness wherever you are.

There are a plethora of reasons why we wind up trapped under the influence of the familiar. This chapter cannot possibly contain them all, because we're complex individuals. However, I attempted to capture as many as possible, in hopes that if this chapter is relevant to you, you'll find your solution in one (or a few) of them. It's not until we identify the problem that we can acknowledge its effect on us and begin to overcome it. I flipped the problems and made them solutions instead.

Roadmap to Victory

First of all, we need to work on the yes/no balance. There's plenty of dialogue out there about the importance of learning to say no. It's critical. Too much giving of ourselves means we have nothing left for ourselves. Our resources—including our time, money, and energy—are limited, so you have to be able to say no if you want to maximize your resources and thus your life. On the flip side, however, you have to also learn how to say yes. As much courage as it takes to be able to say no, it can sometimes take even more to say yes. Have an idea or an opportunity that's outside of your skillset? If it excites you as much as it scares you, go for it! Were you invited to a table where you feel less accomplished than everyone else? Go anyway! This is how we expand, how we release ourselves from the entrapment of the known.

We also need to learn to manage our emotions. Before I expand on this, allow me to point out that emotions aren't positive or negative, good or bad. They just . . . are. It's up to us, however, to learn how to manage them, especially anger, lest they take control of our lives. If you suffer from chronic anger, as described in Chapter 1, then you're too busy being distracted by it to take advantage of your opportunities for growth. The word "awareness" is mentioned a number of times throughout this book, and for good reason. It's the start of change. Before you can alter the situation, you have to be aware of the problem. If you find yourself constantly reacting without thought to things, it is a strong sign that you can use some work in managing your emotions. This basically means realizing that you are not your emotions; they are necessary, but separate from you, and you always have a choice in how you respond as a result of them.

It's important to build self-awareness. What's your motivation for waking up in the morning? What do your values consist of? What are you really good at? What do you struggle with? What do you enjoy? How do you want to feel in this moment? What do you want or need out of life? What activities can you stand to do less of, and which can you stand to do more of? Learning to leverage your gifts and values allows you to get unstuck and create the life you want to live. Otherwise, you'll never know how to apply yourself, overcome your fears, and experience more of what life has to offer.

You also need to stop hanging with the wrong crowd. Hanging out with other trapped people won't free you from your own entrapments. There's no inspiration there. There's no catalyst for change. You have to surround yourself with people who are doing what you want to do, who exhibit the traits and discipline that you aspire to embody as well. If your circle is crowded with negative people, family included, it's time to start doing some adding and subtracting. Add more positivity and release the negatives. The more time you spend with positive people, the more your energy and outcomes will begin to evolve.

There's a story about an eagle that I often tell that pertains to the consequence of hanging with the wrong crowd. It goes: There was once an eagle who didn't know he was an eagle; he thought he was a chicken. He clucked like a chicken, walked like a chicken, and ran with the chickens. The chickens knew that he wasn't a chicken, but he thought he was.

He was out one day walking around, and he saw a great, old bird up high in a tree. That bird looked down and noticed that it was his little son down there.

That was his baby eagle. He went down there and said, "Son, what are you doing down here? You're an eagle."

He said, "No, I'm a chicken."

The father said, "No, you're an eagle. Get up on the building; I want you to jump."

The baby bird got up on the building, jumped, and fell to the ground. He did it again, and fell to the ground a second time. He did it again, and finally, he flew off with the other eagles.

What's the point? The point is, he was an eagle, but he was operating as a chicken. He wasn't in his element. He was out of his environment and with the wrong crowd, so he couldn't access his full potential. Evaluate your circles and, if necessary, do some rearranging.

Stop comparing yourself to other people. There's no winning in this game. There's no such thing as one person doing better than the next; we're all on our own individual path. If you get gratification from feeling that you're doing better than others, then you aren't being motivated to attune your offerings and release your own drawbacks in life. If, on the other hand, you compare yourself to people who you feel are doing better than you, then you'll always feel negative about yourself. Focus on yourself and your own goals, what makes you happy. No competing. No comparing.

Define goals for yourself. There's no progress without a plan. If you haven't defined, and maybe even redefined, goals for yourself, you have nothing to look forward to. Without anything to look forward to, you'll feel like you're on a hamster wheel. Trapped. You'll end up frustrated, angry, or even depressed. It's important to have plans that you can work toward so that you can create your own destiny to work toward and watch unfold.

Check your expectations. At times we set expectations for ourselves that are too high. This is another issue that can stem from childhood. If your parents had very high expectations of you, then you're likely to carry that forward. If you're motivated by making others proud of you, then you're also likely to set unreasonably high expectations of yourself. Sometimes you'll come out on top, but not always. You'll also find it difficult to see the importance of the journey, not just the outcome.

Perfection isn't realistic. You can't expect it from yourself or from anyone else. If you're aiming for perfection, you will never be happy. Let go of the myths and demands of perfection, and stop being afraid of not living up to your own expectations. It causes unnecessary anxiety and sends your mind into fight-flight-freeze mode. The only way you can learn to do something new is by trying and making mistakes.

There's a great African proverb about a lion and a gazelle. You may have heard it before. It says, every morning in Africa, a gazelle wakes up, knowing it must outrun the fastest lion, or it will be killed. Every morning in Africa, a lion wakes up, knowing it must run faster than the slowest gazelle, or it will starve. It doesn't matter whether you're a lion or a gazelle; when the sun comes up, you'd better be running.

The lion's making it happen, he's a beast; he can't afford to linger in his comfort zone for too long. He's trying to take care of his family. He doesn't get up and look at social media and read the newspaper and watch TV. He gets up and he has to go get it, because he knows if he doesn't get up and go get it, his children won't eat. Simultaneously, every day the gazelle wakes up around the same time. When that gazelle wakes up, he doesn't have time to look at Facebook. He has to get moving, because he knows if he doesn't, the lion is going to kill him.

The lion gets up, he's moving. The gazelle gets up, he's moving. They're both on a mission to preserve their life. If that lion can be faster than the slowest gazelle, he's going to have a meal that day. If the slowest gazelle can be faster than the fastest lion, then he's going to be free that day. Now, what would happen if the gazelle was just standing still, not doing anything, idle, trapped in his own fears? He's going to get killed.

When we're idle, it's because we're not being pushed, not being chased. So if you're standing idle in life and you're stuck, that means nothing is pushing you. Nothing is driving you. Nothing is chasing you. Nothing is motivating you for greatness.

Now here's the thing I want to ask you: are you a lion, or are you a gazelle? Either can be good or bad. If you're a lion, what are you chasing? What dream are you chasing? What goal are you chasing? What new known are you seeking? What new life are you looking for? What new thing are you passionate about that you have to pursue? Or are you a gazelle? Is something chasing you, whether something from your past or some demon of the present, is something hunting you down? You know you can't stay still. You know you can't stay stuck. If you stay stuck, you are going to get caught. If you stay stuck, you're going to get eaten up, so you have to keep moving. You have to be about your business everywhere you go. Everything has to have purpose in everything that you do. You have to have a purpose.

Even if it is not healthy, we tend to be comfortable in the known. We don't want to transition to the unknown because we have a fear of the unknown. We may be stuck in one place, stuck in a relationship that is known, because we don't want to jump into the unknown.

When we're stuck, we get comfortable in the known, whether the known is healthy or unhealthy, productive or unproductive, safe or unsafe. We get stuck in a known state because that's all we've known. So when it's time to transition into the unknown, we get stuck. We call it a fear of the unknown. Because if I've transitioned into the unknown, what's my life gonna look like?

If I step out of a relationship, if I step out of an addiction, if I step out of a behavior, I step off the known and familiar and I'm now living in an unknown. I need to figure out how to turn that unknown into my new known, so that my old known becomes my unknown.

Conclusion

Everyone gets trapped under the influence of something at some point in their life. Really, I should have more accurately worded that as "at some *points* in their life," because it happens. When it happens, that influence doesn't care about your career, your income level, your gender, or your ethnicity. It doesn't care about your social status, whether you're educated or uneducated. It doesn't care about your intellect, doesn't care about any of that. Everyone gets stuck, no matter who you are. Life doesn't live on our terms; we live life on life's terms.

Maybe you're stuck in anger or codependency or addiction. Maybe you're wearing a mask right now. Maybe that mask that you're wearing is not really you, and you're putting up a façade to cover up something because you want to be approved of (as we all do).

When I go to different gatherings, whether it's for work, because of family, for church, personal, or social, I tend to put a different mask on if I want people to approve of me, depending on who I want them to see me as. My fear is that they will see me as the real me; I am fearing the unknown. They may not approve of me, so I keep a mask on. But everybody gets trapped. Everybody wears a mask, or has a character issue, or is stuck in some kind of codependent relationship. What matters is how you address that issue.

I want you to know that there is hope for you today. You don't have to stay trapped where you are, but you have to want to change. You have to move past the stuck stage, where you have no desire to change, where people are telling you about your issues but you're not listening.

No matter where you are today, I want you to see where you are and I want you to follow the roadmaps to victory. Despite all of the talking and all of the awareness, real change requires strengthening our will. If I were to sum this entire book up in one word, it'd be will-power. Whether we rely on faith, a memory of feeling empowered by taking a chance, or forcing ourselves to envision a better future, change demands action in the face of discomfort. It demands transcendence, slowing down, and being mindful of our thoughts and behavior.

Regardless of who we believe we are, we have the ability to develop new habits in how we relate to our thoughts, feelings, and behaviors, and in how we relate to others. The strategies here empower us to build resilience and fulfillment in our lives. Freeing ourselves from being trapped under the influence of anger, rigid belief systems, miscommunication, codependency, masks, habits and addictions, and the known and familiar starts with acknowledgement and ends with a choice.

Now that you have the tools, what will your choice be?

Each new hour holds new chances

For new beginnings.

Do not be wedded forever

To fear, yoked eternally

To brutishness.

The horizon leans forward,

Offering you space to place new steps of change.

—Maya Angelou, "On the Pulse of Morning"

ABOUT THE AUTHOR

Brandon Holt is a notable leader. Known for founding the Connect Church of Christ in Baytown, Texas, the internationally acclaimed author of *Preaching Under the Influence: A Minister's Struggle*, changed the way the world views drug use. Beyond the pulpit, Holt serves as a licensed chemical dependency counselor and certified anger resolution therapist, equipping people with life skills to change.

Holt is a trailblazer throughout America facilitating conferences and revivals. His Anger Zone: Breaking the Chains of Chemical Dependency conferences have drawn thousands garnering international attention and landing him on TV shows such as CBS' *The Doctors*, CBN's *700 Club Interactive*, *Great Day Houston*, and *The Gospel Radio Spotlight*. Brandon has also been featured in *Rolling Out Magazine*, *Recovery Today*, and appeared in a cover feature in *His Favor Magazine*. A father of four, Brandon Holt credits his four children as the source of his motivation.

Learn more at brandonholt.org